Beyond the Ring

Uncovering God's Divine Purpose for Marriage, the Role of a Wife, and How to Prepare as a Single Woman

By Amber P. Jones

Table of Contents

Preface

As I sit down to write this book, I'm struck by the irony of my own journey. A journey marked by unexpected twists and turns, moments of clarity and confusion, joy and heartache. Here I am, a single woman, embarking on a mission to explore the intricacies of singleness, drawing from my own experiences and lessons learned along the way.

It wasn't long ago that I found myself on the precipice of marriage, eagerly planning a future with someone I thought was "the one." But just two months before the wedding day, something shifted within me, and I knew deep down that this wasn't the path I was meant to walk. Despite being with a man of God, someone who embodied all the qualities I thought I should desire in a partner, I realized that we simply weren't a match. Our differences in humor, interests, and even values became glaringly apparent, and I knew in my heart that proceeding with the wedding would have been a mistake. In the aftermath of that decision, I found myself grappling with a myriad of emotions. There were moments of doubt and questioning, not about whether it was the right decision, but rather, what was next, am I too old, times when I wondered if my singleness was a punishment or a reflection of my worthiness. I even found myself angry with God, hurt by His seeming silence in the face of my pain.

At one point, I was so hurt and disappointed with God that I decided to take matters into my own hands. I thought I could navigate the complexities of life better on my own, without relying on His guidance. But instead of finding fulfillment and joy, I found myself spiraling into a dark place of severe depression, hurtful relationships, and a profound sense of emptiness; a void that echoed the absence of the one who truly loves me, my Heavenly Father. In my attempt to fill the void with worldly pursuits and fleeting pleasures, I only ended up feeling more lost and alone than ever before. It was a painful realization that trying to live life apart from God's love and guidance only leads to deeper despair and brokenness. It was a humbling experience that taught me the importance of surrendering my will to His and trusting in His perfect plan for my life.

Through it all, there was a quiet whisper of truth; a gentle reminder that God's plans for me were far greater than my own. He wasn't punishing me; He was inviting me into a season of growth, of self-discovery, and ultimately, of deeper intimacy with Him. In the years that followed, I embarked on a journey of healing and transformation, exploring every facet of singleness with an open heart and a willingness to learn. Along the way, I encountered God in ways I never thought possible, discovering His grace, His wisdom, and His unending love in the midst of my brokenness. In the moment of uncertainty and heartache, God spoke to me in a way that I couldn't ignore. He planted a seed of inspiration within me, urging me to share my story and insights with others who might be navigating the complexities of singleness themselves. So, here I am, embracing my own journey of singleness and embracing the opportunity to offer hope, encouragement, and wisdom to those who may be walking a similar path. This book is a testament to the transformative power of God's grace and the beauty that can be found in the midst of unexpected twists and turns. And yes, you heard me correctly, I'm writing this book as a single woman, with a heart full of hope and a story to share. So, whether you're navigating the complexities of singleness yourself or simply seeking a deeper understanding of God's purpose for this season of life, I invite you to join me. Together, let's explore what it means to prepare for marriage, to cultivate intimacy with God, and to embrace the fullness of life that He has in store for each of us.

Introduction

This book breaks away from the mold of traditional "lady in waiting" literature. This book is not about passively waiting for a spouse. Forget everything you think you know about being a wife or waiting for your happily ever after. This book is your guide to ditching the sidelines and stepping into a transformed way of thinking about marriage, singleness, and most importantly, yourself. The core message here is that becoming whole within yourself is essential for contributing to a healthy, Godly marriage. We often hear that relationships require a 50/50 effort, but that's not quite accurate. True partnership starts with two whole people coming together, not halves desperately searching for completion. No one should be burdened with the task of filling a void within the other. Nobody should be your missing puzzle piece. Instead, seek a partner who complements and enhances the amazing woman you already are; someone who cheers you on and makes your strengths shine even brighter.

During the single season, it's vital to prepare for the role of a wife. Let's dig deeper than just the wedding checklists. This is your time to reflect on the kind of wife you aspire to be. This Is the time to nurture the qualities, values, and skills that will contribute to a fulfilling marriage. Rather than viewing singleness as a curse, see it as an opportunity for growth and self-discovery that many overlook. It's not just a waiting period; it's a chance to invest in yourself and deepen your relationship with God. This phase allows you to cultivate inner wholeness and confidence before embarking on a partnership. Many women see marriage as the finish line, but in reality, it's just the beginning of putting into practice everything you've learned while single. That's why it's crucial to enter marriage, as a whole, complete person. This book guides you through this journey of self-discovery and preparation, empowering you to embrace marriage as a fulfilling continuation of your personal growth.

Marriage is like a training ground for both of you, a place where you learn and grow together. It's crucial to shower each other with grace because, let's face it, you're both going to mess up—often. One of the most eye-opening aspects of marriage is how it reveals parts of yourself you didn't even know existed. It's like holding up a mirror to your soul, exposing your flaws and vulnerabilities. In the intimacy of a committed relationship, you're confronted with situations that challenge you in ways you never imagined. It's okay to stumble; it's okay to make mistakes. What matters most is how you respond to those slip-ups. Remember to extend grace not only to your partner but also to yourself. After all, you're both navigating uncharted territory, learning and growing every step of the way. This book isn't just about getting you ready for a healthy, Godly marriage before saying "I do" for life. It's also about helping you tap into your inner strength and purpose, becoming the powerful, purpose-filled woman that God has designed you to be.

This book isn't just a casual read; it's an invitation to embark on a journey of self-discovery and transformation. As you delve into its pages, you'll find yourself challenged to examine your mindset and rethink the way you view marriage and your role as a wife. It's not always easy to confront deeply ingrained beliefs or question societal norms, but I believe that true growth often requires us to step outside of our comfort zones and challenge the status quo. That's why I encourage you not to journey alone. Consider going through this book with friends or fellow single women in your church group. Sharing your thoughts and ideas with others can provide valuable insights and perspectives, and having a support system in place can help hold you accountable as you navigate the sometimes-challenging terrain of self-reflection and growth. Additionally, this book comes with a comprehensive study guide that I urge you to fully engage with. Resist the temptation to simply skim over it; instead, dive deep into its questions and reflections. The goal here is transformation; a shift in your way of thinking that can only come through intentional exploration and introspection. Each section of the study guide is designed to provoke thought and prompt self-examination. Take the time to ponder each question and reflect on your responses honestly. Allow yourself to sit with any discomfort or uncertainty that arises, knowing that it's all part of the process of growth and transformation. By engaging wholeheartedly with the study guide, you'll not only gain a deeper understanding of the material presented in the book but also uncover insights and revelations about yourself and your beliefs.

Chapter 1

Rethinking Marriage

In today's world, our perception of marriage has been greatly influenced by cultural norms and societal trends. Somewhere along the journey of human history, we seem to have lost sight of the authentic meaning and purpose of marriage, trading it for what feels good or seems fitting in our own eyes. In the process, we've buried God's original blueprint for marriage deep within the archives of history. Even though many marriage ceremonies still take place in churches, officiated by pastors, and include references to God, the true significance of the covenant being made before God often gets lost in the whirlwind of wedding preparations and festivities. It's like we go through the motions of a traditional ceremony without fully grasping the depth of the commitment we're making to each other and to God. The sacredness of the covenant can sometimes fade into the background amidst the excitement of the day, leaving it unrecognized and unfulfilled.

In the journey towards marriage, love often takes center stage, and understandably so, it's what draws us together and makes us feel connected. However, what often gets overlooked is the deeper purpose behind the union. Few of us enter marriage with a clear sense of purpose, whether it's understanding our own individual goals or recognizing the greater purpose that God intends for our partnership. We get caught up in the emotions and excitement, sometimes forgetting to pause and consider what God may have in store for us through this union. It's like we're missing out on a crucial piece of the puzzle, unaware of the greater potential and blessings that could unfold if we align ourselves with God's purpose for our lives and relationships.

You'll see me emphasize this point time and time again, marriage is not about you. It was created for a purpose, a divine purpose. Don't get me wrong, while I wholeheartedly believe that marriage can bring immense joy and fulfillment, it's essential to recognize that its primary aim isn't centered around our personal happiness. Let's rewind to the very beginning, to the very roots of creation, when God created the first man. It's the foundation of our human story, filled with divine purpose and meaning, setting the stage for everything that follows.

In Genesis 2:20, after Adam had named all of the livestock, the birds of the air, and the beast of the field, God said there was no one *suitable* for him. The word suitable is defined as appropriate for the purpose. Here, God recognized Adam's need for companionship and created Eve to fulfill the purpose of mankind, encompassing both Adam and Eve. This act of creation laid the foundation for the institution of marriage, which God designed to satisfy the purpose of mankind. So, what is the purpose of mankind?

Looking back at the creation narrative, we understand that God's purpose for mankind was multifaceted. Firstly, God created humanity to cultivate and dominate the earth, and multiply, entrusting them with the responsibility of stewardship over His creation. They were given dominion over every living thing, and the abundance of nature was provided for their sustenance, with only one restriction regarding the tree of the knowledge of good and evil (Genesis 2:17).

The Garden of Eden was Heaven on earth. It symbolized a harmonious relationship between God and humanity, where Adam and Eve enjoyed close communion with their Creator, free from shame or sin. However, the temptation presented by the serpent led to disobedience, resulting in the fall of humanity from grace. This disobedience brought about consequences in the form of curses and separation from God. Yet, in His mercy and love, God provided a solution for redemption through His Son, Jesus Christ. By sacrificing Himself as a sinless offering, Jesus restored the relationship between God and humanity, granting them the authority to fulfill their original purpose, which is still to multiply (in number, resources, and gifts), take back dominion over the earth and occupy until He returns.

Marriage, therefore, is intricately tied to God's overarching purpose for mankind. Rather than being solely for personal happiness, marriage is intended for sanctification, not satisfaction (Ephesians 5-25). Satisfaction is a by-product of a Godly marriage, but not the intended purpose. Understanding the divine intention behind marriage is essential to avoid misusing or misinterpreting its significance. When we lack understanding of the purpose behind something, we often inadvertently misuse it. This concept brings to mind a scene from the Disney movie, The Little Mermaid I used to watch as a little girl. If you have not watched it, I am not advocating that you do, but there is a part in the movie when Ariel finds all these human gadgets underwater and turns to the self-proclaimed wise seagull for answers? But instead of setting her straight, he misidentifies everything, leaving poor Ariel to improvise. Ariel mistakenly used a fork as a hair comb during a dinner scene, much to her embarrassment. Just as Ariel misunderstood the purpose of human objects, individuals must grasp the true purpose of marriage as ordained by God, so it is not misused or abused. By aligning with God's intended design, couples can experience the fullness of His blessings and contribute to His kingdom on earth.

The Greek word for sanctification is **hagiasmos**, derived from **hagiázō**, which means "to make holy." Marriage will expose aspects of yourself that you may not have otherwise known existed. It will reveal areas where you may be selfish, quick-tempered, or lack communication skills. As described in Ephesians 5:22-33, marriage is a direct correlation between Christ and the church and should be modeled accordingly. Let's take a closer look:

[22] Wives, submit yourselves unto your own husbands, as unto the Lord. [23] For the husband is the head of the wife, even as Christ is the head of the church: and he is the savior of the body. [24] Therefore as the church is subject unto Christ, so let the wives be to their own husbands in everything.

As wives, we are to reverence and submit to our husbands in the same way that the church (Christians) is to reverence and submit to Christ. I understand this may be hard to fathom, because not only do we rarely see this modeled within marriages, but we also seldom see it modeled within the church. Many Christians have strayed from having a healthy fear of the Lord. The church has become comfortable with complacency, only willing to submit as far as their comfort level allows. However, we are called to not only proclaim but also to give our bodies as a living sacrifice, holy and pleasing to God, which is our true and proper worship (Romans 12:1).

[25] Husbands, love your wives, even as Christ also loved the church, and gave himself for it;[26] That he might *sanctify* [to

make holy] and cleanse it with the washing of water by the word,[27] That he might present it to himself a glorious church, not having spot, or wrinkle, or any such thing; but that it should be holy and without blemish.[28] So ought men to love their wives as their own bodies. He that loveth his wife loveth himself.[29] For no man ever yet hated his own flesh; but nourisheth and cherisheth it, even as the Lord the church

As wives are to model the church's reverence for Christ towards their husbands, husbands are called to model Christ's love for the church by loving their wives as Christ loves the church. By playing our respective roles, marriage sanctifies us and cleanses us with the washing of water by the word, making us holy, presentable for the return of the Bridegroom, without blemish, spot, or wrinkle. God has given us the blueprint for success, but we have become lost in culture and tradition, learning the "idea" of marriage rather than following God's design. This is why it is crucial to choose a man who is submitted to God, which I will discuss in more depth in later chapters.

[30] For we are members of his body, of his flesh, and of his bones.[31] For this cause shall a man leave his father and mother, and shall be joined unto his wife, and they two shall be one flesh.[32] This is a great mystery: but I speak concerning Christ and the church.[33] Nevertheless let every one of you in particular so love his wife even as himself; and the wife see that she reverence her husband.

Once you enter the covenant of marriage, the two become one flesh. You are now one. Never to be separated. How do you separate one body? So, as you are praying and asking God for a husband, are you ready for this? Are you ready to be submitted to your husband as the church is to Christ? Are you fully submitted to Christ now? If you are not fully submitted to Christ, you will undoubtedly struggle with submission to your husband.

Another purpose of marriage is redemption. Spouses are to help and support one another to stay on their path of spiritual growth and salvation. Ecclesiastes 4:9-12 tells us, **"⁹Two are better than one, because they have a good return for their labor: ¹⁰If either of them falls down, one can help the other up. But pity anyone who falls and has no one to help them up. ¹¹Also, if two lie down together, they will keep warm. But how can one keep warm alone? ¹²Though one may be overpowered, two can defend themselves. A cord of three strands is not quickly broken."**

Marriage serves as a protective barrier against the temptations of sin and the attacks of the enemy. By committing to each other in marriage, couples pledge to remain faithful and honor their covenant with God. This commitment not only guards against the sin of sexual immorality but also empowers couples to stand firm against spiritual warfare. This passage from Ecclesiastes highlights the strength found in unity. When two people come together in marriage, they become stronger together than they would be individually. They can overcome obstacles, defend against adversity, and weather life's storms more effectively when they stand united. One can put one thousand to flight, but two can send ten thousand (Deuteronomy 32:30). A three-strand cord, with God being the third strand is not easily broken. Couples are to be one another's strength, lifting each other up when one falls and providing warmth and protection in times of need. Imagine if more couples entered marriage with a deep understanding of the principles laid out by

God, imagine the strength and power that marriages and couples could embody. Instead, what often happens is couples prioritize their own agendas, driven by their individual needs and desires.

A godly marriage reflects the love and relationship between Christ and His church. Just as Christ sacrificially loves and cares for His bride, married couples are called to demonstrate sacrificial love, selflessness, and forgiveness towards each other. Through their relationship, they can shine as a light in a dark world, showcasing God's love and grace to those around them. A key aspect of marriage is sacrificial love and mutual submission. Both spouses are called to lay down their own desires and preferences for the sake of their partner and the greater good of the marriage. This sacrificial love mirrors the love of Christ, who gave Himself up for His bride, the church. What good does Christian marriages show to the world when we walk away and divorce as soon as times are hard? Christians account for approximately 33% of the divorce rate. How are we using marriage to demonstrate the love of God when we are doing exactly what the world of darkness is doing?

Let's delve a bit deeper into the profound symbolism of Christ as the groom and the church as his bride. Marriage holds such sacred significance that God uses it as a powerful illustration of His love and protective care for us, a truth that often goes unnoticed by many. Jesus himself exemplified the essence of sacrificial love, demonstrating what it means to prioritize the well-being of one's spouse above all else. Throughout the scriptures, we encounter passages that depict the bride (representing the church) being presented to her one husband, Christ. Paul, in his letters, underscores the importance of presenting a bride who is pure and untainted by the allure of worldly distractions (2 Corinthians 11:2-3). Revelation 21:2 paints a vivid picture of a beautifully adorned bride, prepared with utmost care for her husband. It's a piercing reminder of the call to readiness and purity as we anticipate our union with Christ. The Bible offers clear guidance on the significance of preparing ourselves to be presented to our husbands, yet regrettably, many of us fail to take proactive steps toward becoming the pure and holy wives that God desires us to be.

We've been taught the secular idea of marriage. Boy meets girl, they fall in love, get married, have children, and live happily ever after. Marriage is about sacrifice. Marriage requires dying to self, constantly. Marriage is not merely a human institution, but a divine covenant established by God. When couples exchange vows, they enter a sacred covenant with each other and with God. This covenant involves a commitment to stewardship and to fulfill God's purposes for their lives, both individually and as a couple. Marriage, therefore, becomes a vehicle through which God's will is carried out on earth. It should be viewed as a sacred privilege entrusted to us; a responsibility we should cherish and approach with the utmost reverence. Marriage is not about you.

Study Guide: Chapter 1: Rethinking Marriage
This chapter challenges the cultural perspective on marriage and emphasizes its purpose according to the Bible.

Key Points:

- Society often focuses on fleeting emotions like love, while the Bible highlights a deeper purpose for marriage.
- Marriage is a sacred covenant between a couple and God, not just a romantic bond.
- The primary purpose of marriage is to fulfill God's will, which includes stewardship, spiritual growth, and reflecting God's love to the world.

Reflection and Discussion Questions:

1. How has popular culture influenced your view of marriage?

2.   What does it mean for a marriage to be a covenant with God?

3.   How can understanding this concept impact your approach to commitment within a marriage?

4.   How can couples demonstrate sacrificial love towards each other? Give an example. Try to think along the lines of something significant, not just surface level.

5.   Why is preparing for marriage with a spiritual foundation important?

Activities:

- **Reflection**: Write a personal reflection on what you believe is the purpose of marriage.
- **Scripture Study**: Read Ephesians 5:21-33 and Genesis 2:18-25. Discuss the portrayal of marriage in these passages.
- **Communication Activity**: Discuss with your group (or a trusted friend) your expectations for marriage and how those align with a faith-based perspective.

Remember:

- This is a guide to get you started. Feel free to explore the chapter's themes further.
- Personalize your reflections based on your beliefs and experiences.

Chapter 2

Becoming a Wife of Noble Character

Often, when a woman envisions marriage, her mind fills with dreams of the loving husband she hopes to find, the one who will protect, care for, and deeply love her. Yet, amidst these dreams, there's often a gap. We tend to focus less on who we will be for our future spouse, even though that's where our true influence lies, after all, it's the only aspect of marriage we have control over anyway. Have you ever stopped to ask yourself why you want to get married? If your answer isn't rooted in fulfilling God's purposes, you might want to reassess your motivations. Using marriage as an escape from loneliness is a slippery slope. If you're seeking a husband solely to fill a void of loneliness, you will hold him hostage to your personal inadequacies. Your partner shouldn't bear the burden of your insecurities. Before even considering marriage, your life should already be brimming with things that bring you joy and fulfillment. Being single doesn't equate to being lonely. There's a whole world out there waiting to be explored; make friends, travel, experience new things. Don't wait for a husband to complete you; focus on becoming the best version of yourself independently. Give him something to admire that goes beyond just your outer appearance and charm. Become a woman of substance, a woman of value.

The Bible highlights, "When a man finds a wife, he finds a good thing, and obtains favor from the Lord." Here, the key word is "wife," suggesting that one embodies the characteristics of a wife even before officially becoming one. When inquiring about women's perceptions of a wife, the responses often include supporter, helper, and companion. While these qualities are commendable, do they truly encapsulate the entirety of what it means to be a wife? Many women aspire to embody the Proverbs 31 woman without fully comprehending her essence. She is not merely someone who tends to her husband's needs by cooking and cleaning. Let's delve into the scriptures of the Proverbs 31 woman together.

Proverbs 31:10 - "A wife of noble character who can find? She is worth far more than rubies."

The first distinguishing trait of a Proverbs 31 woman is her noble character, often referred to as a "virtuous woman" in some translations. This passage paints a portrait of a woman characterized by high moral values and integrity. When considering the concept of character, one often thinks of qualities such as honesty, trustworthiness, and integrity. Others may associate it with the way one interacts with others, using terms like kindness and consideration. The term "character" originates from the Greek word "kharakter," meaning an "engraved mark," symbolizing an imprint on the soul. Webster's dictionary defines it as "a person's distinctive nature," representing the strength and originality of one's being. Character is not merely something displayed outwardly; it is the essence of who you are.

Being a woman of noble character is defined by your core values and beliefs. Do your beliefs align with the unwavering Word of God? Do you reflect the image of God, characterized by humility and a repentant heart? Perhaps it's time to reassess your beliefs and realign them with God's vision of what a wife should embody. Poor character extends beyond visible traits like untrustworthiness or gossiping; it also includes a lack of self-discipline, self-confidence, or perseverance. Do you find yourself quitting at the first sign of failure or procrastinating on tasks? These are all indicators of poor character. It's essential to acknowledge areas where improvement is needed without dwelling on feelings of insecurity.

The scripture poses the question, "Who can find her?" This question holds a dual meaning. Firstly, it suggests that the search for such a woman requires a man who is set apart, guided by discernment and wisdom. Secondly, it implies that a woman of this caliber can only be found under the protective care of the Father. The likelihood is slim that these individuals would cross paths in a nightclub setting. This isn't to say they must meet at church, but rather, through a journey of singleness where both parties allow God to shape them into reflections of Himself, aligning their speech, actions, and thoughts with His divine will; their paths may intertwine in due time.

She's worth far more than rubies, and she knows it. She carries herself with a quiet strength, not desperate for acceptance from others. She's secure in who she is, an embodiment of confidence without a hint of arrogance. Confidence, she understands, isn't about competing with others; it's about embracing her uniqueness. While arrogance boasts, "I'm better than you," confidence simply declares, "I am different from you." She doesn't feel the need to impress anyone because she's comfortable in her own skin. There's no need for her to try to entice or charm, confidence naturally radiates from her being. She's not just pretending to be herself; she authentically lives it.

***Proverbs 31:11 - "Her husband has full
confidence in her and lacks nothing of value."***

This scripture highlights just how vital a woman's trustworthiness is in her husband's eyes. He relies on her abilities, judgment, and overall character, entrusting her with the significant task of managing their household and making sound decisions. The fact that he feels lacking in nothing of value or importance suggests that her presence enhances their family life, bolstering her husband's endeavors and contributing to their shared prosperity. But how does a husband-to-be gauge these qualities in his partner before tying the knot? As mentioned earlier, you embody the essence of a wife long before officially taking on the title. During the time of courtship and singleness, he keenly observes your actions and choices. How do you manage your time and finances? Is your home a haven of order and cleanliness? And when it comes to the kitchen, does your culinary prowess shine, or do you find comfort in the convenience of takeout meals? These are the everyday aspects of life that he pays close attention to, as they provide valuable insights into your character and readiness for marriage. Through these observations, he begins to form a picture of the partner you'll be, recognizing the qualities that will strengthen your bond and build a life together. So, even before saying "I do," the journey of discovering each other's strengths and compatibility has already begun.

I want to clarify that I'm not suggesting the woman's role in the household should always revolve around cooking and cleaning. That's something for you and your husband to decide together. However, he does appreciate seeing that you can maintain a well-organized and tidy home. These are skills you can start honing now. If you're not confident in your cooking abilities or if your idea of dinner involves opening a can of soup and grabbing a bag of chips, consider taking some cooking classes. It could be a fun and enjoyable activity to do with your girlfriends while also improving your culinary skills.

Proverbs 31:12- "She brings him good, not harm, all the days of her life."

This line really hits home about how a wife's actions and intentions shape the tone of her relationship with her husband over time. It's all about consistently finding ways to uplift and support him, whether it's in the things she says, the things she does, or the choices she makes. That means refraining from airing out their disagreements to friends and family or speaking negatively about him behind his back. Instead, it's about protecting his dignity and reputation, even in the heat of the moment. In essence, it paints a picture of a wife who embodies love, support, and respect in her interactions with her husband. She prioritizes his well-being and creates a safe space where he feels valued and appreciated.

Ladies let's talk about confiding in others about your relationship, whether you're dating or married. Running to your mom or girlfriends to vent negatively about your husband or partner might seem like a quick fix, but it can create more harm than good. During the dating phase, it's crucial to find someone mature and unbiased to confide in; preferably someone in a healthy marriage who can offer you sound advice. However, try to avoid confiding in family members, as their forgiveness might not come as easily as yours, potentially causing tension between your family and your partner. Your girlfriends don't need to know every detail of your relationship either. Your partner should always feel protected, not like he's being side eyed at gatherings because of a disagreement you've had. Once you're married, it's beneficial to find a couple you both trust to confide in. Having a supportive, trustworthy confidant can make all the difference in navigating the ups and downs of married life.

> *Proverbs 31:13-19 - "[13]She selects wool and flax and works with eager hands. [14]She is like the merchant ships, bringing her food from afar. [15]She gets up while it is still night; she provides food for her family and portions for her female servants. [16]She considers a field and buys it; out of her earnings she plants a vineyard. [17]She sets about her work vigorously; her arms are strong for her tasks. [18]She sees that her trading is profitable, and her lamp does not go out at night. [19]In her hand she holds the distaff and grasps the spindle with her fingers. [20]She opens her arms to the poor and extends her hands to the needy. [21]When it snows, she has no fear for her household; for all of them are clothed in scarlet. [22]She makes coverings for her bed; she is clothed in fine linen and purple."*

This woman is an absolute powerhouse! She's not just a businesswoman; she's a force to be reckoned with. She's out there making deals, buying land, and turning it into something incredible. She's a skilled worker who's constantly striving to perfect her craft. And let me tell you, she's not waiting around for anyone to hand her success, she's creating it herself. Even for a man who wants to provide financially for his wife and family, there's something undeniably attractive about a woman with ambition and drive. She's a multitasking marvel, effortlessly juggling multiple roles and responsibilities. She rises early in the morning, before the break of dawn, setting the tone for the day ahead for both her and her family. It's not uncommon for her to steal a quiet moment alone with God while her loved ones are still lost in slumber, pouring out her heart in prayer.

By the time they awaken, she's already in motion, preparing breakfast to nourish their bodies and souls, she's the ultimate caretaker. What's truly inspiring is that amidst her hectic schedule, she still finds time to connect with her husband at the end of the night. She's not just focused on her own goals; she's always thinking about how she can make life better for those around her. She's the epitome of strength, grace, and compassion—a real-life hero in every sense of the word.

> **Proverbs 31:23 - "Her husband is respected at the city gate, where he takes his seat among the elders of the land."**

Being with a woman of her caliber requires a certain kind of man. A man of authority and influence in his own right. Together, they make quite the power couple, complementing each other perfectly. I can just picture him at the city gates, chatting with the other guys, and when the topic of wives comes up, he stands out. While others may grumble about their wives' attitudes or laziness, he simply can't relate. His wife's virtue and strength set her apart from the rest, and it's evident in the way he carries himself and speaks about her. A man is respected by other men based on how his wife represents him primarily through her actions, demeanor, and character. When a man's wife conducts herself with grace, integrity, and kindness, it reflects positively on him, as it suggests that he has made a wise choice in his partner. When a man's wife demonstrates a strong sense of loyalty and commitment to her husband, it enhances his standing among his peers. Conversely, if a man's wife behaves in a manner that is disrespectful, unkind, or dishonorable, it can diminish his reputation and respect among others. Ultimately, a man's wife is seen as a reflection of his judgment, character, and values.

> *Proverbs 31:25-31- "[25]She is clothed with strength and dignity; she can laugh at the days to come. [26]She speaks with wisdom, and faithful instruction is on her tongue. [27]She watches over the affairs of her household and does not eat the bread of idleness. [28]Her children arise and call her blessed; her husband also, and he praises her: [29]Many women do noble things, but you surpass them all. [30]Charm is deceptive, and beauty is fleeting; but a woman who fears the Lord is to be praised. [31]Honor her for all that her hands have done, and let her works bring her praise at the city gate.*

"Clothed in strength and dignity" speaks volumes about her character. It's more than just a description, it's a reflection of her inner resilience and integrity. She faces the future with confidence and optimism, exuding a wisdom that others naturally gravitate towards. Instead of wasting time on idle gossip or getting caught up in Reality TV drama, she invests her energy into meaningful pursuits that uplift her family and community. She is appreciated and praised by her family and community. She's not just honored and respected; she's a shining example of what it means to be a God-fearing wife.

Those are some big shoes to fill, but these are the attributes of a God-fearing wife. This statement really hits home, doesn't it? Being a God-fearing wife isn't just about fulfilling a checklist of duties; it's about embodying qualities of strength, dignity, wisdom, and respect within the context of marriage and family life. It's like realizing the incredible responsibility and privilege that comes with being a wife who deeply respects and honors her faith. It acknowledges the high standard set by the Proverbs 31 woman and the challenge it presents to live up to such virtues. Do you still think you're a Proverbs 31 woman? I hope so.

Study Guide: Chapter 2: Becoming a Wife of Noble Character

This chapter explores the characteristics of a wife according to the Bible, emphasizing a Christ-centered approach.

Key Points:

- Focus on becoming a wife who reflects God's character, rather than seeking marriage to fulfill a void.
- A wife's core values and beliefs should align with God's word.
- True confidence comes from embracing your uniqueness and living authentically.
- A wife should be trustworthy, supportive, and a source of strength for her husband.
- Cultivate skills and manage your household effectively.
- Strive for good character, not just outward appearances.

Reflection and Discussion Questions:

1. How does popular culture portray wives differently from the Proverbs 31 woman?

2.   What are your strengths and weaknesses in developing the qualities of a Proverbs 31 woman?

_____

_____

_____

_____

3.   How can you cultivate a deeper trust and respect for your future spouse?

_____

_____

_____

_____

4.   What does it mean to be "confident" without being arrogant?

_____

_____

_____

_____

5.   How can wives create a safe and supportive space for their husbands?

_____

_____

_____

_____

Activities:

- **Character Inventory:** Write down your core values and beliefs regarding marriage and roles within the marriage. How well do they align with the teachings of the Bible?
- **Skill Development:** Identify areas where you'd like to improve your skills, like cooking or finance. Plan ways to develop them.
- **Communication Challenge:** Discuss with your group (or a trusted friend) your views on the Proverbs 31 woman and how they can apply to your future marriage.

Remember:

- This is a guide for personal reflection and growth.
- Focus on your journey of becoming a wife who honors God.

Chapter 3

Submission in Marriage- A Godly Perspective

1 Peter 3:1 - "¹Wives, obey [respect] your own husbands. Some of your husbands may not obey the Word of God. By obeying your husbands, they may become Christians by the life you live without you saying anything. ²They will see how you love God and how your lives are pure."

God has entrusted us with a powerful mandate: to respect our husbands. While husbands are called to love their wives, as wives, our primary task is to show them respect. After all, God understands the innermost needs of His children because He created them. As women, we long to feel loved and cherished, to be treated with tenderness and care. While men certainly appreciate love, their deepest desire is often to feel respected, valued and honored for who they are. Respect means recognizing your husband's leadership role and allowing him to guide the family. It doesn't mean you can't voice your opinions or offer advice, but it does mean trusting his decisions, even when they differ from your own. Grant him the grace to make mistakes, just as God grants us grace time and time again. When he does make a wrong decision, as he inevitably will, your affirmation and encouragement will go a long way in fostering unity and partnership in your marriage. It creates a safe space where he doesn't have to be perfect but can grow and learn alongside you. Criticism, chastisement, or emasculation have no place in a healthy marriage. Instead, maintain a gentle and quiet spirit, grounded in obedience to God. Your husband's heart will be won over not by your words, but by your consistent example of faithfulness and reverence for the Lord. It's a humbling realization that your recourse for guiding your husband towards righteousness lies in prayer and trust in God's sovereignty.

Marriage is a journey of sacrifice and continual selflessness. It's not for the faint of heart or immature. Before entering this sacred covenant, it's crucial to understand that love alone is not enough. Marriage demands a willingness to endure, even when love falters, and a readiness to lay down one's own desires for the sake of the union. It's a profound commitment, one that requires courage, maturity, and a deep understanding of what it truly means to love sacrificially. In 1 Peter 3:6, we're reminded of Sarah's exemplary behavior towards Abraham, where she honored him by referring to him as "lord." This wasn't just a term of endearment, it signified acknowledgment of his authority, power, and influence within their household. Now, let's pause and think for a moment, how many of us modern women would feel comfortable addressing our husbands in such a manner? It's understandable if the idea feels a bit foreign or even unsettling. Yet, Sarah's example teaches us that true respect and submission doesn't diminish our power; they elevate it.

It's important to note that a husband who is submitted to God won't abuse or misuse the honor and respect shown to him. Just look at Abraham, while he held the authoritative role in their household, we see in Genesis 16:2 that he yielded to his wife's influence when he agreed to father a child with Hagar. This instance is just one example among many in Scripture where husbands heeded their wives' counsel, even if it wasn't necessarily the wisest decision. It's a reminder that women possess significant influence over the men who love them. But with great influence comes great responsibility. It's crucial for women to avoid manipulating or basing their actions solely on emotions. Instead, we should strive to use our influence wisely and with integrity, always seeking the best interests of our partners and our relationships. After all, true influence isn't about controlling others, it's about guiding and supporting them in love and mutual respect. Contrary to popular belief, honoring your husband with respect and obedience doesn't make you weak; it empowers you. There's strength and liberation in submission, not because it diminishes you, but because it aligns you with God's design for marriage. A woman who carries the fear of God in her heart and places her trust in Him alone is a force to be reckoned with. She isn't just an ordinary woman, she's extraordinary. And guess what? So are you.

Remember, marriage isn't just about you, it's about something far greater. As a wife, your role as a "help meet" goes beyond simply being there for your husband; it's about uplifting, encouraging, and supporting him as God continues His perfect work within him. It's crucial to remember that your husband is first and foremost a child of God before he is your spouse. God's desire for his growth and transformation far surpasses your own. Likewise, as a daughter of God, you are cherished and loved beyond measure. God longs to lavish you with the boundless love of Christ, fulfilling the desires of your heart in ways you couldn't even imagine. So, when you commit to your marriage vows, you're not just pledging to fulfill your own desires or aspirations, you're dedicating yourself to carrying out God's purpose for your life and your union with your husband.

Every action, every word spoken, every moment shared within your marriage should be done with a heart devoted to serving the Lord. In doing so, you'll find fulfillment and satisfaction beyond anything you could have ever dreamed of. After all, when God is at the center of your marriage, His blessings know no bounds. As a wife, your commitment to God's plan for your marriage isn't dependent on whether your husband fulfills his role as expected. That's why it's so important to choose a partner who not only hears God's voice but also follows His lead. When you marry someone who shares your spiritual values and commitment, you're laying down a strong foundation for a marriage rooted in faith and shared beliefs. Finding a husband who walks hand in hand with God means you're both on the same page when it comes to your journey of faith. It's not about finding someone flawless, but rather someone who's willing to grow spiritually alongside you. This mutual pursuit of God strengthens your relationship and prepares you to face life's ups and downs with resilience and grace. In the end, marrying a man who prioritizes his relationship with God creates a marriage where God's love and wisdom are central. It's this deep connection that helps you weather any storm and build a lasting bond that stands the test of time.

Study Guide: Chapter 3: Submission in Marriage- A Godly Perspective

This chapter explores the concept of wifely submission from a Christian perspective, emphasizing respect and spiritual growth.

Key Points:

- A wife's primary responsibility is to show respect to her husband, even if he doesn't follow God.
- True respect involves trust and allowing your husband to lead, while offering your opinion.
- A wife's Christ-like character can influence her husband towards God.
- Marriage requires sacrifice, maturity, and a deep understanding of love.
- Respect and submission empower a wife and don't diminish her influence.
- Choosing a spouse who shares your faith strengthens the marriage foundation.

Reflection and Discussion Questions:

1.   How does this chapter challenge cultural perspectives on wifely submission?

2.   What are some ways to show respect to your husband, even when you disagree?

_____

_____

_____

_____

3.   How can a wife maintain a gentle spirit while also offering her perspective?

_____

_____

_____

_____

4.   How can couples grow spiritually together?

_____

_____

_____

_____

Activities:

- **Bible Study**: Read 1 Peter 3:1-7 and Ephesians 5:21-33. Discuss how these passages portray husband and wife roles.
- **Communication Challenge**: Discuss the importance of shared faith in a marriage.
- **Prayer Exercise**: Pray and ask God to reveal to you the areas you need to grow in now that will ultimately help you to fulfill the role as a wife.

Remember:

- This is a guide to explore God's design for marriage.
- Focus on growing in Christ.

Chapter 4

Choosing a Godly Husband

Choosing your husband takes Godly discernment. Yes, you choose your husband. It is not like cavemen days where the man "finds" a woman, hits her over the head and drags her back to his home by her hair and forces her to become his wife. Neither does God select one person in the entire world to be your husband. God respects our freedom of choice, and the idea of a predestined partner contradicts the essence of free will that He has bestowed upon us. God will never come between man and his ability to choose. Reflecting on the story of the Garden of Eden, some wonder why God would place the tempting tree in Adam and Eve's midst. Yet, it's a powerful symbol of God's respect for our autonomy and capacity to make choices. By presenting the option to disobey, God granted us the freedom to navigate our own paths and make decisions, shaping our journey of faith and accountability in profound ways.

I once had a conversation with a deeply "religious" woman who firmly believed in the concept of predestined marriages. She believed God preselected one person for each of us. I couldn't help but wonder about the implications of free will, so I asked her what would happen if one person decided to "disobey" and marry someone else instead. Her response, that the other person would be destined to remain single for life, sounded a bit far-fetched to me. If I'm being completely honest, it sounds absurd. Don't get too caught up in the notion of finding your predestined soulmate or worrying about whether "the one" is still out there waiting for you. Trust that in due time, God will bring suitable options into your life. Instead of fixating on the idea of a perfect match, focus on living your life to the fullest and nurturing your relationship with God. As you continue to grow and develop personally, you'll find that God will guide you towards individuals who are compatible with your values and aspirations. Trust in His timing and His plan for your life, knowing that He will lead you to the right person when the time is right. It's important to maintain patience and openness to the possibilities when they arise. Ultimately, the decision of who to marry is yours to make.

While God doesn't handpick your spouse for you, He does provide guidance on what to look for in a partner. He often works through our choices and discernment. Let's start by addressing a common stumbling block, stop missionary dating! This is when we enter relationships with non-believers, hoping to lead them to faith through romantic involvement. Not only does it not work but often leads to other complications. The Bible asks, "What does a believer have in common with an unbeliever?" (2 Corinthians 6:15). Instead, it's crucial to evaluate potential partners based on their alignment with our faith and values. Regardless of their background or upbringing, what truly matters is their personal relationship with God. It doesn't matter that he grew up in church and his grandmother was an evangelist. Is he saved? Does he display the qualities of Godly character? Is he actively seeking spiritual growth through Christ and bearing the fruits of the Spirit? Does he demonstrate a willingness to listen to God's guidance and follow His will? If you find that a potential partner doesn't meet these criteria, it's essential to recognize that the relationship might not lead to the kind of healthy, God-honoring partnership you desire. Likewise, if you discover areas where you fall short, it's a chance for personal growth and spiritual development as you move forward on your path to marriage.

It's common to encounter Christian men at different stages of their spiritual journey, and they may not always be as advanced in their walk with God as you are. However, this shouldn't automatically lead to dismissing them altogether. Many may not have experienced or understood what a close relationship with God truly entails, especially in a landscape where modern churches may not always exemplify it. But here's the thing: it's not your responsibility to hold his hand and guide him through his spiritual growth. I strongly advise against taking on that role. Instead, allow him the space to navigate his own journey. If he's genuinely interested in being with you, he'll show it by taking steps to grow in his faith and align himself with God's will. Don't just settle for empty words or promises. Use discernment to observe whether there are tangible changes in his actions and character. Has he demonstrated genuine growth and maturity in his "fruit," the evidence of his faith? Is he willing to submit to the guidance of strong male leadership in his life? These are important considerations as you discern whether he's the right match for you spiritually.

In the end, it's about more than just finding a husband; it's about becoming the wife that God desires you to be. This means continually striving to align yourself with His will and values, both in your relationships and in our own personal journey of faith. Don't fall into the trap of being a martyr in your relationships. It's not noble to enter a romantic relationship with the intention of leading someone to Christ. Despite how pleasant he may seem; the reality is that you have fundamentally different beliefs and values. As 1 Corinthians 15:33 warns, "Bad company corrupts good character," and your core identity is at risk of being compromised. Attempting to build a relationship on such contrasting spiritual foundations will inevitably lead to discord and disharmony. As Amos 3:3 points out, "Can two walk together, unless they are agreed?" The foundational differences in your beliefs will create ongoing tension and conflict, leaving you both feeling unsettled and disconnected.

While you may believe you're doing good by trying to lead him to Christ, the truth is that your integrity and character are being compromised in the process. By compromising your convictions to be with him, you're sending a message that your faith is negotiable. A woman of noble character cannot be swayed or compromised in her values and beliefs. A man of integrity understands that when it comes to marrying a woman, he must first seek the approval of not just the woman herself, but also her Father. This means presenting his case before her Father, demonstrating why he believes he is worthy of marrying His daughter. Any man worthy of you should get the approval of your Heavenly Father for your hand in marriage, as well as your earthly father. Thankfully, God's criteria for a suitable partner are clearly outlined in His word. There's no need to constantly seek divine revelation or pray for confirmation about whether a particular man is right for you. God's spoken word, or Rhema, will always align with His written word, or Logos. So, if a man doesn't meet the standards set forth in Scripture, there's no need to hesitate or second-guess. Trust in God's wisdom and guidance, knowing that His plan for your life is perfect and His timing is always right.

While foundational characteristics like devotion to God are essential qualities to seek in a potential husband, they alone are not sufficient when making the final determination on compatibility. Being a devout Christian doesn't automatically guarantee a perfect match. God desires the best for us, including in our relationships. He understands the importance of physical attraction and intimacy within marriage. It's natural to struggle with engaging intimately with someone to whom we feel no attraction. It's not about having a checklist of superficial traits; it's about finding someone who genuinely resonates with you on a deeper level. Someone whose presence brings out the best in you and whose company you genuinely enjoy. So, while it's important to share core beliefs and values, don't feel pressured to force a connection with someone simply because they align with your faith. Trust in God's guidance and timing, knowing that He has someone special in mind who will not only share your beliefs but also captivate your heart in ways you never imagined.

Imagine being in a relationship where your partner's sense of humor just doesn't click with yours, and laughter feels forced instead of natural. That's not the kind of fulfilling connection that God wants for you. He wants your relationship to be filled with genuine joy and deep connection, where laughter comes easily and strengthens your bond. It's totally fine to have specific desires when it comes to your future husband. You can pray for someone who's tall, good-looking, funny, and successful. But it's also important to ask God for guidance on a deeper level. Instead of just focusing on surface-level traits, ask Him to help you see your potential partner through His eyes. Look beyond the surface and think about qualities like responsibility, integrity, and kindness. Does he keep his promises? Does he manage his time and money wisely? Is he someone who treats others with respect and generosity? These are the qualities that really matter, showing the kind of person God trusts with His blessings. Remember, true wealth isn't about flashy cars or expensive clothes; it's about having a heart that's in line with God's values. So instead of being swayed by superficial signs of success, focus on what truly matters, your potential partner's character, values, and relationship with God. As my Apostle would say, "Don't look at what he drives, but rather, what drives him." So, don't stress over what's in his bank account. Remember, true wealth does not come from man, but God Himself. He's the one who grants the ability to create wealth (Deuteronomy 8:18).

Understanding your partner's vision is like having a roadmap for your relationship journey. Without it, you might end up feeling lost or unsure of where you're headed. That's why it's totally okay to dig deep and ask your partner about their dreams and goals. What does he envision for your future together? What are his aspirations for your family? Don't be afraid to have these conversations; if he's scared off by your curiosity, it might be a sign that he's not the right match for you. A man without vision cannot lead you. It's important to find a partner whose vision aligns with yours, someone you can confidently submit your own dreams and goals to. Entering marriage with conflicting visions only leads to division and discord. It's crucial to understand that it's not biblical for a man to submit to your vision simply because he may not have one of his own. That's not how the divine order is designed. According to scripture, a man is called to lead his family, and to do so effectively, he must possess a clear vision. In turn, as his partner, you must be willing to align your vision under his leadership. While both partners should have a say in decision-making, it's important for the man to step up and provide that guiding vision.

If we go back to the story of creation in Genesis 2, we see that the instruction regarding the tree of the knowledge of good and evil was given solely to Adam. It was his responsibility to communicate this directive to his wife, Eve. Even after they sinned in Genesis 3, when God called out to Adam, asking, "Where are you?" It was Adam who was held accountable. God didn't address Eve directly, highlighting Adam's role as the leader entrusted with upholding the vision set forth. Unfortunately, in many modern marriages, the breakdown occurs when women take the lead, often because men haven't been taught how to fulfill their role as leaders. But your story doesn't have to follow this pattern. Trust that there is a man of God destined to lead you in alignment with God's vision for your life and your relationship. It's important to note that even if the woman is the primary breadwinner in the family, the man is still called to have a vision for their household. This doesn't change the dynamic of leadership within the marriage. According to biblical principles, the man is entrusted with the responsibility of leading the family, regardless of financial roles. This doesn't diminish the woman's contributions or value within the partnership. Rather, it emphasizes the importance of each spouse fulfilling their respective roles in alignment with God's design for marriage. So, regardless of who earns the primary income, the man is still called to provide vision and leadership, while the woman is called to support and submit to his guidance.

Let's talk about visions for a moment. Do you have a clear picture of where you want to go in life, or are you waiting to jump on the bandwagon of someone else's star? Now, don't get me wrong, being willing to support your husband's vision is super important. But you must have a vision for your own life too. You should be a totally whole individual, with dreams, goals, and passions that are uniquely yours. You understand the purpose for your life and you're actively pursuing it, whether Mr. Right has shown up on the scene yet. Because here's the truth, you never know when your spouse will arrive. So, what are you doing in the meantime? Instead of sitting around twiddling your thumbs and waiting for Prince Charming to sweep you off your feet, use this time to invest in yourself and your future? Take that class you've been eyeing, start that business you've been dreaming about, or volunteer for that cause that's close to your heart. Don't put your life on hold just because you haven't found your happily ever after yet. Having a vision for your life isn't just about achieving your goals, it's about becoming the best version of yourself, for yourself. It's about embracing your God-given potential and making the most of every moment, whether you're single or married. So go ahead, dream big, chase those dreams, and trust that everything will fall into place in its own perfect time. After all, the best love stories often unfold when you least expect them to.

It's understandable to be excited about encountering a potential romantic interest after a prolonged period of singledom. However, it's imperative to maintain a level-headed approach amidst this newfound enthusiasm. You see, it's perfectly natural to feel a surge of excitement in the presence of someone who piques your interest. However, it's vital to temper that excitement with a healthy dose of discernment. It's all too easy to get swept up in the moment, to see a glimmer of charm or kindness and hastily declare, "This must be the one!" Instead of jumping in feet first, take your time to really get to know this person. If something feels off or gives you pause, don't brush aside those concerns just because you've been waiting for a while. Resist the temptation to settle for the first option that comes your way, like grabbing the little "teddy bear" behind door #1. Instead, have faith in God's plan, even when you can't see the bigger picture.

Embrace the mindset of the three Hebrew boys who declared, "My God will come through, but even if He doesn't, I will not compromise." Adopting this attitude means being fully committed to living a life without compromise, regardless of the circumstances. Trust that God has something greater in store for you, even if it's behind door #3 and you can't see it yet. Surrender yourself to the journey of unwavering faith and trust in His perfect timing and provision. Watch them closely, observe how they interact with others, and pay attention to how they handle life's ups and downs. Are they consistent in their actions and words? Do their values and beliefs align with yours? Resist the urge to just dive into the depths of infatuation. Instead, savor the unfolding of each moment, allowing the bond between you to grow organically. Trust in the process, and trust in yourself to navigate it with wisdom and grace.

One common danger I've observed among many women is fixating on a man they may not even be dating, sometimes someone they've never even met. They become infatuated with this person, projecting their ideals onto them and assuming they must be "the one." Some have even gone to the extent of telling them, "God told me you're my husband. "But let's take a moment to pause and reflect on this. It's crucial to remember that God doesn't override anyone's free will, so if He truly revealed this person as your future spouse, trust that He has or will do the same for them. God doesn't need us to play matchmaker; He's quite capable of orchestrating divine connections Himself. I've also seen situations where women believe that another woman's husband is meant to be theirs. However, this goes against God's commandment: "You shall not covet your neighbor's spouse."(Exodus 20:17). If you've ever found yourself in this position, it's crucial to repent and let go of any thoughts of coveting. If you have ever prayed to God for another woman's husband, repent, and renounce your agreement with witchcraft. Trust that He has a plan for your love life, and His timing is always perfect. By staying faithful and obedient to Him, you'll pave the way for His blessings to unfold in your life.

Imagine a king, a father, determined to find the perfect match for his beloved daughter, knowing her worth exceeds any earthly treasure. He meticulously assesses potential suitors, rejecting each one deemed unworthy. His daughter, eager but patient, watches as her father discerns the hearts of men. "Daddy, this one seems promising," she exclaims, hopeful. But the king, her father, sees beyond surface success, knowing true love requires more than mere accomplishments. Again and again, she points to men she deems suitable, only to be gently redirected by her discerning father. He knows her better than anyone, understanding the intricacies of her heart and the depth of her desires. Finally, after much anticipation, a suitor emerges who embodies the virtues of her father. He carries himself with the same grace, possesses the same strength of character, and shares her father's unwavering love and commitment. The father couldn't wait any longer to introduce his daughter to the man he believed embodied the virtues he held dear. With excitement, he brought the suitor home to meet his daughter.

As they talked, laughed, and shared stories, the father couldn't help but notice the similarities between the suitor and himself. They both had a similar sense of humor, a shared passion for helping others, and a deep-rooted commitment to family. It was clear to the father that this man truly cared for his daughter and would cherish her as he did. After the visit, as they said their goodbyes, the father couldn't contain his excitement. He pulled his daughter aside and shared how impressed he was with the suitor, expressing his hopes that she felt the same connection he did. With a smile, he reassured her that he only wanted her happiness and that he believed this man could provide it. Seeing her father's genuine approval and excitement filled the daughter with a sense of warmth and reassurance. She trusted her father's judgment and felt grateful to have his support as she explored this new relationship.

You see, her father's discernment was not just about finding any match; it was about safeguarding her legacy of royalty. She carries within her the bloodline of kings and queens, destined to break generational curses and restore honor to her lineage. For those who resonate with this story, understand that you too carry a legacy of royalty within you. You are destined for greatness, tasked with the noble responsibility of shaping the future of your bloodline. So, if you find yourself waiting for the right partner, trust in the wisdom of your Heavenly Father. He is protecting your legacy, ensuring that you are yoked with someone who not only honors your worth but also aligns with your divine purpose. You are going to produce and multiply salt in the earth. Not only from your womb, but your influence. Trust your Father. Trust in His timing, for He knows the desires of your heart and is guiding you towards a union that will multiply blessings and bring glory to His name.

Study Guide: Chapter 4: Choosing a Godly Husband
This chapter explores how to choose a husband through faith and discernment, emphasizing God's will and personal growth.

Key Points:

- Don't focus on finding a predestined soulmate; focus on your relationship with God.
- Choose someone who shares your faith and values.
- Avoid "missionary dating" - don't date someone hoping to convert them.
- Look for a man who demonstrates Christ-like qualities and is growing spiritually.
- Don't settle for someone who doesn't meet your standards.
- Don't compromise your faith in a relationship.
- Seek a partner who is compatible with you on multiple levels.
- God's will for your partner is revealed in the Bible.
- Look for qualities like responsibility, integrity, kindness, and a shared vision.
- The man is called to have a vision and lead the family, while the woman supports.
- Trust God's timing and plan for your love life.

Reflection and Discussion Questions:

1.   How does this chapter challenge traditional views on finding a spouse?

2.   What are some qualities you are looking for in a future husband?

3.   How can you discern if someone is genuinely growing in their faith?

4.   How can couples develop a shared vision for their future?

_____

_____

_____

_____

Activities:

- **Prayer:** Pray for guidance in discerning God's will for your future spouse.
- **Journaling:** Reflect on your own values and goals for your future.
- **Discussion:** Have an open conversation with a trusted friend or mentor about your dating life (if applicable).

Remember:

- This guide is to help you choose a spouse based on your faith.
- Focus on growing your relationship with God and becoming the best version of yourself.

Chapter 5

Embracing Singleness as a Gift

Many women find themselves asking, "Why hasn't it happened for me, what's wrong with me?" or "Why does it seem like everyone else is finding love except me?" These are valid questions to what you're feeling, ones that don't always come with easy answers. But one thing remains certain: marriage is a desire placed in our hearts by God. While some, like the Apostle Paul, are graced to be single, most of us feel a deep longing for partnership. If you've been waiting for your future husband for what feels like an eternity, I won't bombard you with clichés, or beat you over the head with Bible verses or tell you to just have more faith. Trust me, I understand how frustrating and discouraging it can be to hear those words. The truth is, I don't have all the answers as to why you're still single, but I can offer some guidance on how to navigate this season of waiting. First and foremost, remember that singleness is a gift, not a curse. By embracing this period of waiting as an opportunity for personal growth and self-discovery, you can find fulfillment and joy even amid longing for a partner. Instead of viewing waiting as torture, see it as a time to cultivate your relationship with God, pursue your passions, and invest in meaningful friendships and community. In 1 Corinthians 7:34 Apostle Paul says as a single woman you only have to be concerned with the affairs of God, whereas a married woman also has to consider the affairs of pleasing her husband. Focus on becoming the best version of yourself, both spiritually and emotionally, so that when the right person does come along, you'll be ready to embrace the next chapter of your life with confidence and grace. And above all, trust in God's timing and His perfect plan for your love story. He knows the desires of your heart, and He will fulfill them in His own time and in His own way.

How you perceive and approach being single can truly shape your experience during this season of your life. Once you find yourself happily married, surrounded by your beautiful family, you'll inevitably find yourself reminiscing about this season of your life. It's a common sentiment among married individuals; there are aspects of singleness that you'll miss, even though you wouldn't necessarily want to change anything about your current situation. So, while you're in this season of being single, embrace every moment with joy and gratitude, knowing that it's a unique chapter in your life that will shape your journey towards marriage and beyond.

Our beliefs are like a GPS that navigates our lives. If you find yourself believing that God is intentionally withholding marriage from you or overlooking you, I urge you to reconsider your perspective. How we choose to perceive a situation greatly influences our attitude and behavior. When we believe that God is treating us unfairly, it can lead to feelings of resentment or impatience, tempting us to take matters into our own hands or even turn away from God altogether. But the truth is, God is not withholding His blessings from you. He is a loving Father who desires the best for His children. He promises in Psalms 84:11 that He withholds no good thing from those who walk with integrity.

He longs for you to receive every promise He has made to you, including the gift of marriage. If you feel burdened by past mistakes and believe that God is punishing you, I want to reassure you that God's desire is not to punish but to redeem you. He longs to restore and renew you, offering forgiveness and grace without reservation.

To truly grasp the heart of God, it's essential to cultivate an intimate relationship with Him. This means setting aside time to connect with Him through prayer and immersing yourself in His Word. It's in these moments of intimacy that He unveils His deepest truths and whispers His secrets to your soul. Shifting your mindset is key to aligning yourself with God's perspective. One effective way to do this is by cultivating an attitude of gratitude. Practicing gratitude not only uplifts your spirits but also helps dissolve bitterness and negativity. Each night, take a moment to jot down something you're thankful for from the day's experiences. Challenge yourself to find something new to appreciate each time. It's like finding little gems in the midst of everyday challenges. Now, let's talk about mindset shifts. Let's compare Fixed and Growth Mindsets. In a Fixed Mindset, bumps in the road can feel like roadblocks, but with a Growth Mindset, they're more like detours leading to new opportunities. Consider these examples:

Fixed Mindset: "I failed my test. I won't pass this class."

Growth Mindset: "I failed my test. I'll seek help from a tutor and study harder to succeed."

Fixed Mindset: "My family has a history of health problems due to being overweight. I'll probably face the same fate."

Growth Mindset: "My family has a history of health problems, but I can break the cycle by adopting healthy habits and prioritizing my well-being."

Embracing a Growth Mindset empowers you to navigate life's challenges with resilience and optimism, knowing that every setback is an opportunity for growth and transformation. Choosing to see setbacks as steppingstones instead of stumbling blocks is what it's all about. A growth mindset is not denying your reality but denying the finality of that reality. It's about recognizing your power to shape your reality by speaking life into it, just as Romans 4:17 teaches us. You can change your reality simply based on how you think. Don't succumb to a defeated mindset just because things haven't unfolded as quickly as you'd hoped. Instead, anchor yourself in God's promises and keep pressing forward toward your destiny. Remember, His timing may not always align with yours, but that doesn't mean your breakthrough isn't on its way.

Let me clarify something important: I'm not suggesting you simply plaster a smile on your face and try to see the world through rose-colored glasses. What I'm advocating for is a deeper, more profound shift in your mindset—a transformation from the inside out. Positive thinking, while well-intentioned, often skirts the surface, merely skimming over deeper issues and emotions. It's like putting a band-aid on a wound without addressing the underlying infection. True transformation, on the other hand, involves digging deep into our core beliefs and challenging the lies we've internalized over time. Have you ever met someone who seems like the epitome of positivity until life throws them a curveball? Suddenly, their sunny disposition fades. That's because their positivity is merely a facade; deep down, their core beliefs remain unchanged. And when the storm hits, their true colors emerge. This is why superficial attempts at positivity, like reading self-help books or attending seminars, can only take you so far. Without genuine transformation at the core level, our newfound optimism crumbles when confronted with real challenges. Transformed thinking, however, delves beneath the surface, reshaping our perspectives, attitudes, and behaviors from the inside out. It's not about putting on a show of positivity; it's about rewriting the narrative of our lives, replacing falsehoods with truth, and embracing a mindset that withstands the fiercest storms.

My perspective on singleness shifted dramatically when I began to see it as a gift from God. A season of growth and preparation for what lies ahead. Despite knowing that God desires marriage for me, I've come to appreciate the freedom and independence that comes with being single. There are days when all I crave is some quiet time to myself, to unwind and recharge without any distractions. And in those moments, I'm grateful for the opportunity to focus solely on my own needs, knowing that this season won't last forever. I understand that soon enough, I'll have the privilege and responsibility of considering the needs of a partner as well. But for now, I'm embracing this time of learning and self-discovery. God is revealing to me valuable insights about marriage, the purpose of partnership, and the qualities to look for in a future husband. Looking back, I realize how ill-equipped I would have been to choose a partner if I had rushed into things without this understanding. I would have made mistakes, likely selected the wrong person and misunderstanding the true purpose of marriage. Now, armed with knowledge and wisdom, I'm better positioned to not only build a happy marriage but to fulfill the role of a wife as God intended. I'm grateful for this season of singleness, knowing that it's preparing me for the beautiful journey that lies ahead.

I have friends who married young, and while their marriages are rooted in faith and love, they've admitted that navigating the journey of matrimony at a more mature stage could have spared them from unnecessary challenges. They've faced their fair share of bumps and bruises along the way, leaving behind scars that needed time to heal. It's easy to envy those whose lives seem picture-perfect from the outside, but what we often overlook are the unseen struggles they've endured. Behind their smiles lie stories of perseverance and resilience, of overcoming obstacles and learning from mistakes. Consider the hidden blisters on their feet, before you consider walking in their shoes. Instead of longing for someone else's journey, find the blessings in your own path and express gratitude to your Heavenly Father for it. He sees the bigger picture and knows what's best for you, guiding you through experiences that will shape and strengthen you for the road ahead.

Study Guide: Chapter 5: Embracing Singleness as a Gift
This chapter explores the concept of singleness as a time for growth and preparation for marriage, emphasizing a positive and grateful perspective.

Key Points:

- Singleness is a gift from God, not a curse.
- Embrace this time for personal growth, self-discovery, and pursuing passions.
- Focus on your relationship with God and becoming the best version of yourself.
- Trust God's timing and plan for your love life.
- Shift your mindset from negative to gratitude.
- Cultivate a growth mindset that sees challenges as opportunities.
- True transformation involves addressing core beliefs and replacing negativity with truth.
- Singleness allows for freedom, independence, and focusing on personal needs.
- This season equips you with knowledge and wisdom for future marriage.
- Be grateful for your journey and trust God's plan.

Reflection and Discussion Questions:

1.   How can you reframe your perspective on being single?

2.   What are some ways to cultivate a growth mindset?

_____

_____

_____

_____

3.   How can you practice gratitude during challenging times?

_____

_____

_____

_____

4.   What is the importance of self-discovery during singleness?

_____

_____

_____

_____

Activities:

- **Journaling:** Reflect on your current beliefs about singleness.
- **Gratitude List**: Make a daily list of things you're grateful for.
- **Self-discovery Activity**: Explore your hobbies, interests, and passions.
- **Bible Study**: Read scriptures about God's plan and timing.

Remember:

- Singleness is a season of preparation for marriage.
- Focus on your relationship with God and personal growth.
- Trust in God's timing and perfect plan for your life.

Chapter 6

The Power of Your Words and Beliefs

The Bible teaches us that faith has the power to shape our reality, much like the word of God framed the creation of the world (Hebrews 11:3). Similarly, our words serve as small rudders guiding the course of our lives (James 3:4-6). They possess the remarkable ability to bring blessings or curses into existence (Proverbs 18:21). Imagine your subconscious as a vast expanse of quicksand. When words are spoken, they initially rest on the surface, but with repetition and acceptance, they sink deeper into your subconscious, shaping your beliefs, whether positively or negatively. These beliefs form the bedrock of your mindset, influencing how you perceive yourself and the world around you. Whether your mindset leans toward growth or remains fixed can significantly impact your interpretation of yourself and the situations you encounter. Embracing a growth mindset allows you to navigate challenges with resilience and optimism, while a fixed mindset may hinder your ability to adapt and thrive. Recognizing the power of your words and beliefs is the first step toward shaping a mindset that aligns with your aspirations and empowers you to live a fulfilling life.

When you speak negatively about your life or situations, even in jest, you're essentially charting the course of our own journey. Have you ever caught yourself saying, "I'm never getting married," or perhaps more seriously, "there are no good men out there"? These seemingly harmless statements can have a profound impact. By vocalizing them, we unknowingly align ourselves with their negativity, allowing them to seep into our subconscious and shape our perspective. Before we know it, we're embracing these falsehoods as truths, fostering a pessimistic outlook that breeds blame and resentment. This blame game serves only to distract us, trapping us in a cycle of frustration and stagnation where solutions remain elusive. What started as a passing joke now exercises power over your thoughts and emotions, steering you away from the abundant life you desire. Your words, whether spoken in jest or earnestness, carry significant weight; they hold the power to shape your reality. By speaking the words of God over your life, you can redirect your trajectory toward His promises. As you consistently affirm His truths, they take root deep within you, anchoring your faith and guiding your decisions. Instead of dwelling on anxious thoughts or false narratives, declare the goodness of God and His faithfulness to fulfill His promises. So, replace every lie you've embraced with the truth of God's Word. Affirm His promises daily, proclaiming His provision, His companionship, and His care over your life. As you do so, you command authority to shape your destiny according to His perfect plan.

Paying attention to our own words is crucial, but it's equally important to be mindful of the words and influences we allow into our lives from the outside. These influences can come from various sources such as friends, family, television, social media, and more. Take a moment to reflect on the conversations you engage in or the content you consume. Do they uplift and enrich your life, or do they drag you down? Remember, you are responsible not only for the words you speak but also for what you choose to listen to. If you entertain gossip or negativity, you're contributing to its spread and its impact on your own mindset. Consider the parable of yeast (Matthew 13:33), think about the last time you watched a movie that left you feeling inspired or listened to a podcast that made you think differently about the world. Just like the way yeast works its magic in dough, those stories and words have a way of working their way into our hearts and minds, shaping our thoughts, beliefs, and actions. But just as easily as positive influences can uplift us, negative ones can bring us down. Imagine if you added just a pinch of spoiled yeast to a batch of dough, it would ruin the whole thing. In the same way, negative words and influences can taint our hearts and minds, leading to doubt, fear, or division.

That's why it's so important to be mindful of what we listen to and watch. By choosing stories and influences that uplift and inspire us, we can cultivate a positive and empowering inner world. Whether it's the music we listen to, the books we read, or the shows we watch, each choice has the power to shape our lives in profound ways. So, let's remember the lesson from the parable of yeast. Just as we carefully select the ingredients for our favorite recipes, let's also carefully choose the influences that shape our thoughts, beliefs, and actions. By nourishing ourselves with positivity, wisdom, and truth, we can spread goodness and light and transform our lives for the better. You can't aspire to embody the qualities of a Proverbs 31 woman while immersing yourself in the toxic drama of reality television, where disrespect and dishonor are normalized. To truly reflect the image of God and align yourself with His character, you must saturate your heart and mind with His truth and goodness. Fill your thoughts with what is noble, pure, and uplifting, as Philippians 4:8 advises. As you do, you'll find that your language begins to reflect this transformation, and you become less tolerant of negativity and toxicity in your surroundings.

Study Guide: Chapter 6: The Power of Your Words and Beliefs

This chapter explores the power of words and beliefs in shaping your reality and achieving your goals, with a focus on aligning your mindset with God's promises.

Key Points:

- Words have the power to shape your reality, both positively and negatively.
- Negative self-talk and beliefs can hinder your growth and fulfillment.
- Speak God's word over yourself to build faith and trust in His plan.
- Be mindful of external influences like media and negativity from others.
- Choose uplifting and inspiring content to nourish your spirit.
- Align your thoughts and actions with God's character and promises.

Reflection and Discussion Questions:

1.   What are some negative phrases you've used about yourself or your situation?

2. How can you challenge those negative beliefs with God's truth?

_____

_____

_____

_____

3. What impact does media and social media have on your thoughts and emotions?

_____

_____

_____

_____

4. How can you cultivate a more positive inner world?

_____

_____

_____

_____

5.　　What examples of media uplifts and inspires you?

_____

_____

_____

_____

6.　　How can you cultivate a more positive media diet?

_____

_____

_____

_____

Activities:

- **Word Fast**: Identify a negative word/phrase you commonly use and avoid saying it.
- **Daily Confessions**: Write down positive affirmations based on God's word and repeat them daily.
- **Media Audit**: Track your media consumption for a week and identify areas for improvement.
- **Content Replacement**: Choose uplifting content (books, podcasts, music) to replace negativity. If you're not sure if it's negative, ask yourself, would Jesus enjoy it?
- **Gratitude Journal**: Focus on things you're grateful for to cultivate a positive mindset.

Remember:

- Your words and beliefs have power.
- Choose to speak and think according to God's promises.
- Surround yourself with positive influences for a fulfilling life.

Chapter 7

Holiness: A Life Transformed

When we talk about holiness, especially during seasons of singleness, the focus often shifts solely to sexual purity. And while maintaining sexual purity is undoubtedly crucial, it's essential to recognize that holiness encompasses much more than that. Holiness is about aligning our hearts and minds with God's, living in harmony with His will and His values. Think of holiness as a lifestyle, a habit of being in sync with God. It's not just about our actions; it's about our identity and who we are at our core. Holiness means sharing God's heart, embracing what He loves, and detesting what He hates, as Romans 12:9 reminds us. Rejecting sin is a fundamental aspect of holiness, but it goes beyond simply abstaining from sinful behaviors. It means distancing ourselves from anything that compromises our spiritual purity, even in the form of entertainment or influences that contradict God's truth. So, as you navigate your single season, remember that holiness is a holistic pursuit. It's about cultivating a deep connection with God, embodying His character, and making choices that reflect His values in every aspect of your life.

Holiness is often viewed as a prerequisite for entering heaven, a ticket to an afterlife of eternal bliss. While this is true, holiness also has a profound impact on the quality of our lives here on earth. Let me explain why. Holiness fosters a deeper connection with God. Holiness is one of the keys that unlocks

Heaven to operate on your behalf. Before God shares His most intimate revelations with us, He often puts us through tests to ensure that we are fully committed to living a life of integrity and faithfulness. He wants to bless us abundantly, but He also wants to know that we won't misuse or waste the blessings He entrusts to us. Pursuing holiness isn't just about following a set of rules; it's about building a deep, unwavering trust between us and God. When you embrace holiness, you show God that you are willing to surrender your life completely to Him. You demonstrate your commitment to living in alignment with His divine principles and values. And as you prove yourself faithful in the small things, God begins to entrust you with greater responsibilities and blessings. Think of it like this: you are a reflection of God Himself, and He wants to protect His investment in you. By walking in holiness, you not only honor God but also position yourself to receive His abundant blessings. It's like opening the floodgates of heaven and allowing God's goodness to pour into every area of your life. There's a standard for walking closely with God and receiving His very best. God isn't a respecter of person; He's a respecter of principles. Honor the principles He has established for a fruitful and fulfilling life. As you pursue holiness, keep your eyes fixed on the standard set by God's Word, knowing that He is faithful to fulfill His promises to those who seek Him with all their hearts.

I don't want you to confuse holiness with legalism. It's not about rigidly following rules like a checklist or striving to meet a standard through sheer willpower. Instead, it's about being so deeply connected to the Holy Spirit that your very desires start to shift. Imagine going on a strict diet and cutting out certain foods for an extended period. When you try to reintroduce those foods later, your body rejects them, right? It's the same in the spiritual realm. Initially, it requires discipline, but as you become more filled with the Holy Spirit, your cravings change. You no longer must force yourself to avoid certain things; you naturally recoil from them. The environments you once found comfortable start to feel suffocating. Your taste for worldly pleasures diminishes, and certain conversations or relationships begin to feel unsettling. People might notice a change in you and question it, even criticize it, saying, "you've changed.", or "You think you're too good for us now." In the words of Dr. Stacy LeMay, "I am not too good for you, but I am too good for *this*." You see, you can't straddle the fence between God and the world. God calls this lukewarmness, and He finds it repugnant (Revelation 3:15-16). He wants you to make a choice, to be all in or all out. And here's the thing: everything the world offers; God can provide in abundance and with eternal value. But you must decide to leave behind the empty promises of the world and embrace the riches of God's kingdom.

Turning away from the allure of the world and wholeheartedly pursuing God is a deeply humbling journey, one that often comes with its own set of challenges and sacrifices. It's not always the most popular path to take, and you may find that not everyone in your life understands or supports your decision. In fact, some of the people you care about the most may not be able to accompany you on this journey. It's a difficult realization to face, but you can't wait for others to catch up or join you. You must move forward, even if it means going alone at first. Trust that those who are meant to walk alongside you will eventually find their way, but in the meantime, you must press on. It's natural to feel a sense of loneliness or isolation as you step out in faith but remember that God is always with you. He sees every step you take, and He promises to never leave you nor forsake you. Even in the moments when it feels like you're walking alone, trust that God is there, filling in the gaps and guiding you every step of the way.

Consider this powerful truth from James 4:4: God identifies anyone who aligns themselves with the world as an enemy. Yes, you read that right, an **enemy**. God sees it as a declaration of enmity. It's a sobering realization, isn't it? There's no such thing as finding a "balance" between the world and God. You must choose. You must decide whether to cling to the fleeting pleasures of this world or embrace the abundant life God has prepared for you. It's not about finding a middle ground or trying to find loopholes to satisfy worldly desires with spiritual ones. That's a trap many fall into. Many Christians, including some prominent Christian figures, try to justify worldly living under the guise of being relatable or culturally relevant, but that's not what God desires. But you don't have to be among them. Instead, look to the ultimate example: Jesus Christ. He walked this earth, fully human yet entirely sinless. He showed us what it means to live in alignment with God's will, to resist the temptations of the world, and to find true fulfillment in the Father's love. So, when faced with the choice between worldly allure and heavenly riches, follow in the footsteps of Christ. Choose the path of righteousness, knowing that in God's kingdom, you'll find everything your heart truly desires.

I want to make it clear that striving for perfection isn't the goal here. You're human, after all, and you're bound to make mistakes along the way. However, what's crucial is maintaining a heart posture of repentance, an attitude of humility and a willingness to acknowledge your faults and shortcomings.

Immediate repentance is key. It's about catching yourself in those moments where you have fallen short, whether it's in your actions, words, or even your thoughts, and making a conscious decision to turn away from them right then and there. It's not just about uttering a quick apology; it's about sincerely shifting your mindset and behavior to align with God's will. For me, this means making repentance a daily habit. Every night before I go to bed, I take a moment to reflect on my day and ask God to reveal any areas where I may have missed the mark. If something comes to mind, I don't hesitate, I repent immediately, seeking God's forgiveness and guidance to help me grow from my mistakes. In those times when I can't pinpoint anything specific to repent for, I still take a moment to acknowledge any potential blind spots and trust God to reveal them. It's all about staying open to His guidance and being willing to address any areas where you may have fallen short, even if you're not fully aware of them yet. By embracing this practice of immediate repentance, you open yourself up to God's transformative work in your life. It's a humbling process, but it's also incredibly freeing. Instead of carrying the weight of your mistakes, release them to God.

When you sin, God does not get mad *at* you, He gets mad *for* you, because He knows the destructive path sin can lead you down. God's heart isn't filled with anger towards you; it's filled with compassion. Understanding the consequences of your actions, when you open the door to sin, you're essentially giving the enemy permission to wreak havoc not just in your life, but in the lives of those around you, even future generations. But here's the truth: God isn't interested in condemning you; He's interested in redeeming you. He wants to cleanse you from your sins and heal your wounds. No matter what mistakes you've made, there's nothing that can separate you from God's love (Romans 8:31). He's not waiting to punish you; He's waiting to embrace you with open arms. For some of you, it's hard to comprehend this kind of unconditional love, especially if you've never experienced it from your earthly parents. But God's love transcends human understanding. It's a love that knows no bounds, a love that never gives up on you. So, even when it feels like the weight of your mistakes is too heavy to bear, remember that God's love is greater. Trust Him, lean on Him, and allow His love to wash over you and set you free from guilt and shame.

To truly reflect the likeness of our Heavenly Father, we must first know Him intimately. This means carving out intentional time for prayer, diving into His Word, and even incorporating periods of fasting into our routine. Building a daily habit of communication with God is essential; an ongoing conversation that nurtures our relationship with Him. Consider setting aside a dedicated time each day to retreat to a quiet space and commune with God. For some, this might mean rising early before the demands of the day take over. By prioritizing this time with God, you demonstrate the same level of commitment and intentionality that you would expect from a loving partner in marriage. Just as you will cherish moments of connection and conversation with your future spouse, so too should you eagerly anticipate your encounters with your Heavenly Father. Whether it's through prayer, worship, reading Scripture, or simply sitting in His presence, be open to the leading of the Holy Spirit. Sometimes, it may be a moment of quiet reflection; other times, it might involve singing, praying fervently, or even dancing before the Lord. The key is to show up, ready to engage with God and willing to follow wherever His Spirit leads.

When it comes to spending time with our Heavenly Father, it's important not to approach it too rigidly, like just another item to check off your to-do list. While scheduling time for it can be helpful to ensure you prioritize, because adulting can get busy, the goal is to cultivate a deeper intimacy with God where you genuinely desire to be in His presence. Sure, you may already talk to Him throughout the day, but there's something uniquely special about setting aside moments of uninterrupted, distraction-free time to simply bask in His presence. It's in these quiet moments that God often chooses to reveal His most intimate secrets, sharing His love and wisdom in profound ways. So, while it's good to have structure in your prayer time, also strive for a level of intimacy with God where spending time with Him becomes a cherished opportunity rather than just another task to complete.

Fasting involves intentionally abstaining from food for a set period, prioritizing spiritual nourishment over physical sustenance. It's a powerful act of self-denial, where you subdue the desires of the flesh and elevate your connection with God. In the Bible, we see fasting as a profound expression of humility and submission. King David, for instance, spoke of humbling himself through fasting (Psalm 35:13), recognizing its significance in deepening his relationship with God. Moreover, fasting isn't merely about depriving oneself of food; it's about positioning oneself to hear from God clearly. Moses, during his fast on Mount Sinai, received divine revelations (Deuteronomy 9:9-18), and Daniel's fasting led to profound insights and answers (Daniel 10). Furthermore, fasting is a spiritual battleground, a form of warfare against the forces of darkness (Matthew 17:21). It's also a form of intercession, as seen in Queen Esther's fasting on behalf of her people (Esther 4). However, fasting must be coupled with consecration, setting oneself apart for God's purposes. Merely abstaining from food without a genuine dedication to seeking God's will can be likened to going hungry without purpose. It's about redirecting the time and resources typically spent on meals toward prayer, worship, and serving others, aligning oneself with God's heart and purposes (Isaiah 58).

Fasting is like hitting the reset button for your soul; it's how you intentionally humble yourself before God. We see this practice echoed throughout the Bible, from David in the Psalms to Daniel in the book of Daniel. Both recognized the power of fasting as a way to humble themselves before God. But what exactly does humility have to do with intimacy with God? Well, that's everything. Humility opens the door for you to draw closer to Him, to pour out yourself so that you can be filled with more of Him. It's in those moments of surrender, when you set aside your own desires and comforts, that you create space for God to work in your life in powerful ways. And here's the thing, humility isn't just about emptying yourself; it's also what gives you the strength to pursue holiness. When you humble yourself before God, you're admitting that you need His help to live a life that honors Him. It's a recognition that you can't do it on our own, but with God's help, you can overcome any obstacle and grow closer to Him each day.

Fasting isn't the only path to humility, but it's a powerful one. When I talk about humbling yourself, I'm really talking about letting go of your own desires, ego, and pride to make room for God's will in your life. This can happen in various ways, through acts of repentance, forgiveness, and more. But fasting stands out because it directly confronts your fleshly desires. Think about it:

when you fast, you're deliberately saying no to your physical needs and desires. By denying yourself in this way, you're reminding yourself that there are greater things at play, namely, your spiritual growth and relationship with God. Fasting is not just about depriving yourself; it's about redirecting your focus. When you give up something that you crave, it creates space for you to turn your attention to God and seek His presence more intentionally. It's a way of saying, "God, I want more of You in my life, even if it means sacrificing something that feels good in the moment." Fasting is a surefire way to kill fleshly desires and draw closer to God.

Understanding the difference between fasting and consecration is key to fasting successfully. Fasting, as you mentioned earlier, involves intentionally abstaining from food for a specified period. It's about denying ourselves physically to seek God more fervently. Consecration, on the other hand, is about setting yourself apart for God's purposes. It's not just about fasting from food; it's about abstaining from anything that might hinder your relationship with God or lead us away from His will. This could include things like TV, social media, or other distractions that take your focus away from Him. Fasting should always be accompanied by consecration. Think about it like the parable of yeast, you can't purify your body through fasting if you're still allowing impure influences to enter through your eyes and ears. It's like trying to clean a cup while continuing to pour dirt into it. So, when you fast, it's important to also consecrate yourself; to set yourself apart completely for God's purposes. That means being intentional not only about what you're abstaining from but also about what you're allowing into our hearts and minds. By purifying both your body and your thoughts, you create a more fertile ground for God to work in your life and draw you closer to Him.

The concept of fasting is a lifestyle rather than just a once-a-year event. While many may participate in occasional fasts with their church or community, the Bible speaks of fasting as a consistent practice, a way of life. It's a deeply personal journey, and the frequency and duration of your fasts should be guided by your relationship with God and His leading in your life. By making fasting a regular part of your life, you're committing to a lifestyle of self-discipline and spiritual growth. It's a way of actively seeking God's presence and aligning yourself with His purposes daily. Incorporating fasting into your life can also have profound benefits for your relationships, including your marriage. Fasting teaches the value of submission and selflessness, qualities that are essential for a healthy and thriving marriage. As you learn to submit to God through fasting, you'll find that submission in your marriage becomes less of a burden and more of a privilege, a beautiful expression of love and partnership.

Study Guide: Chapter 7: Holiness- A Life Transformed
This chapter explores the concept of holiness as a lifestyle choice, emphasizing its impact on your relationship with God and overall well-being.

Key Points:

- Holiness is more than just sexual purity; it's about aligning your life with God's will.
- It fosters a deeper connection with God and unlocks His blessings.
- Avoid negativity and influences that contradict God's truth.
- Pursue holiness through daily choices and a surrendered heart.
- Embrace a lifestyle of repentance and immediate course correction.
- God's love is unconditional, even when you make mistakes.
- Cultivate intimacy with God through prayer, scripture, and fasting.
- Fasting is a form of self-denial to deepen your spiritual connection.
- Consecration involves setting yourself apart for God's purposes.
- Integrate fasting into your life for continuous spiritual growth.

Reflection and Discussion Questions:

1.   How have you traditionally viewed holiness?

2.   What areas of your life need to be brought into alignment with God's will?

3.   How do you identify with the concept of immediate repentance?

4.   Share experiences of God's forgiveness and love.

5.   How can you dedicate more time for prayer and Bible study?

6.   What are some ways you can incorporate fasting into your life?

Activities:

- **Personal Inventory**: Identify areas where your actions or habits contradict God's principles.
- **Media Consecration**: Choose a specific media source to abstain from for a set period.
- **Daily Devotional**: Set aside dedicated time for prayer and scripture reading.
- **Gratitude Journal**: Focus on things you're grateful for to cultivate a positive mindset.
- **Fasting Challenge**: Start with a short, simple fast and gradually increase duration.

Remember:

- Holiness is a journey of aligning your thoughts, actions, and desires with God's will.
- Embrace God's forgiveness and unconditional love.
- Develop a lifestyle of prayer, scripture, and intentional time with God.
- Fasting is a powerful tool for spiritual growth and intimacy with God.

Chapter 8

Healing From Emotional Traumas

It's unfortunate that many women have endured various forms of trauma by the time they reach adulthood. Whether it's physical, emotional, or sexual abuse, or experiences of rejection, the pain runs deep. To anyone who has suffered I want to start by saying whatever the source of your hurt and pain, I want to extend my heartfelt apologies. I'm sorry. I'm sorry for the hurt you've endured. I apologize on behalf of the ones that hurt you. You did not deserve it. It was not your fault, and for that I am sorry. You are not what happened to you. You are not defined by the pain you've experienced. You *are* good enough. You *are* smart enough. You *are* worth it. You *are* enough. You are valuable beyond measure. I believe that with every ounce of my being, and I hope you do too. While you may not be responsible for the traumas inflicted upon you, it is your responsibility to heal from them.

Healing is a journey, not a destination that you reach overnight. It's a process that unfolds gradually over time. While God is the ultimate healer, seeking support from a therapist can also be incredibly beneficial. Having someone grounded in the Word of God to guide you through your healing journey can provide invaluable support and insight. True healing often requires revisiting painful memories and emotions that you've pushed aside or buried deep within. It's like moving into a new home but finding that many rooms are closed off because they're filled with unpacked boxes from the past. God desires for you to experience complete healing, not just partial restoration. God says, "You are the light of the world. A town built on a hill cannot be hidden. Neither do people light a lamp and put it under a bowl. Instead, they put it on its stand, and it gives light to everyone in the house. In the same way, let your light shine before others, so that they may see your good deeds and glorify your Father in heaven." (Matthew 5:14-16).

Will you make the choice to swing open the doors of your heart, and begin to unpack those emotional boxes and reclaim the fullness of life that He intends for you? Allowing the light of God's love to flood in and illuminate every hidden corner? It won't be easy. Opening those doors may stir up old wounds and emotions, causing discomfort and pain. There may be moments when you're tempted to shut them tight again and retreat to the safety of darkness. But I urge you, don't give in to that temptation. The journey of healing, though challenging, is worth every step. You don't have to continue living under the weight of pain, fear, and distrust. God promises freedom, liberty, and peace in the very place where you dare to open up and let Him in. In that sacred space, His consuming love stands ready to burn away all that is dead and broken, replacing it with His divine restoration and wholeness. So, take a deep breath, summon your courage, and let the healing light of God's love flood into every corner of your heart.

Healing is like wiping clean the lenses through which you see life and people. Imagine stepping into marriage with murky lenses; you wouldn't see your husband's intentions clearly. Even his sincere gestures might trigger memories of past hurts, distorting your perception. For instance, if your ex only showed affection after causing pain, you might question your husband's kindness, wondering if there's an ulterior motive. At first, you might appreciate his efforts, but doubts could creep in. Eventually, you might find yourself questioning his actions, inadvertently pushing him away. As time goes on you may begin to question why he isn't affectionate like he used to be. It's a vicious cycle born from unresolved pain. That's why it's vital to heal and gain clarity, not just for yourself, but for your future spouse too. Clear vision sets the stage for genuine connection and a deeply fulfilling relationship.

The first step to healing from emotional healing is acknowledging your pain. Allowing yourself to become aware of your pain is like turning on the light in a dark room, it's the first step to seeing things clearly. We often try to brush aside our hurts, plastering on a smile and saying, "I'm fine," but deep down, the pain lingers, waiting to be addressed. It's like having a scab over a wound; if you scratch it, the wound beneath is exposed once again, vulnerable and raw. Ignoring your pain may offer temporary relief, but it doesn't lead to true healing. Instead, it leaves you susceptible to being triggered repeatedly, like reopening an old wound. It's essential to confront your emotions head-on, allowing yourself to feel the hurt, sadness, or anger without judgment. Just as a scar serves as a reminder of a healed wound, acknowledging your pain allows you to recognize your past hurts without letting them control you.

By facing your pain honestly and openly, you create space for true healing to occur. It's not about blocking out the pain or pretending it doesn't exist; it's about acknowledging it, allowing yourself to grieve, and ultimately, moving forward with a newfound sense of strength and resilience. Journaling can be a powerful tool as you navigate through the maze of emotions. It's like having a private conversation with yourself, a safe space where you can pour out your thoughts and feelings without fear of judgment. When you sit down to journal, be specific, dig deep and explore the who, what, and why behind your pain. How did it make you feel? Anger, often the surface emotion, can be a mask for deeper feelings like hurt, betrayal, or fear. Take the time to identify the root cause of your emotions.

Reflect on the impact this pain has had on your life. Has it left scars that still ache? Has it shaped the way you view yourself or others? Acknowledging the ripple effects of your pain can be a crucial step toward understanding and healing. In your journal, you have the freedom to express yourself fully. Write down everything you wish you could say to the person who hurt you. Be honest, raw, and vulnerable. This isn't about seeking revenge or confrontation; it's about releasing the weight of your emotions and finding closure within yourself. This journal is for your eyes only; a sacred space where you can lay bare your heart before God. Allow yourself to be as detailed and specific as you need to be. In doing so, you're not only processing your emotions but also inviting God into the depths of your pain, trusting Him to guide you toward healing and wholeness.

Next, forgive. Forgiveness is often misunderstood as letting someone off the hook or excusing their behavior. You're not excusing or minimizing what they've done; rather, you're choosing to release the hold that bitterness and resentment have over your heart. It's like unlocking the chains that have kept you bound to the past, freeing yourself to move forward with a lighter spirit and an open heart. The reason why God tells us to forgive immediately is because unforgiveness is like a seed planted in soil, and when left unaddressed roots begin to grow. Roots of bitterness. The roots spread and the tree begins to grow, branches begin to form, then it starts to produce fruit. However, not sweet, juicy fruit like the fruits of the Spirit, but rather rotten, bitter fruit like, jealousy, envy, anger, fear, divisiveness, gossip, backbiting. Meanwhile, the person who wronged you may be going about their lives, unaffected by your bitterness. You may convince yourself that withholding forgiveness is a form of punishment, but you're only punishing yourself.

Forgiveness isn't just about letting others off the hook; it's about setting yourself free. When you hold onto anger and resentment, you're the one who suffers most. It's like carrying around a heavy burden that weighs you down and prevents you from fully embracing the present and future. By choosing to forgive, you're reclaiming your power and choosing to no longer be defined by your pain. It's important to remember that forgiveness is a process, not a one-time event. You may need to forgive the same person multiple times as new layers of hurt surface or old wounds resurface. And that's okay, it's all part of the healing journey. Continue to verbally affirm, "I forgive [name] for [specific offense], and I bless them, and I release them." Even if you don't feel it initially, continue declaring forgiveness until it becomes a reality in your heart and mind. As you extend forgiveness to others, you're also opening yourself up to the possibility of trust and vulnerability once again. It's like clearing away the debris of the past to make room for new growth and connection in your relationships. Forgiveness isn't easy, nor does it require reconciling with those who hurt you or give them another chance to cause pain. But it's a necessary step in breaking free from the torment of past hurts. Holding onto grudges only allows the tormentor to continue their hold over you through memories that replay in your mind.

Finally, it's important to be kind to yourself throughout the healing process. Everyone goes through emotional wounds, and it's perfectly okay to not be okay sometimes. Accepting that healing takes time and that setbacks are part of the journey is crucial. Patience and grace are key. Healing is not a linear process; it has its ups and downs. So, be patient with yourself as you navigate through these moments. Treat yourself with compassion, just as you would a close friend going through a tough time. Allow yourself the space and time you need to heal fully and completely. During your healing journey, it's important to remember that you are not alone. God is right there with you, holding your wounded heart gently in His hands. He understands the pain you're going through, and He's actively working to bring healing and restoration to your wounded soul. Think of God as a skilled craftsman, carefully smoothing over the calloused areas of your heart and turning them into tender flesh once again. His presence is a safe refuge, a place where you can pour out your heart and find solace in His comforting embrace. You can trust Him to guide you through the healing process and lead you into a place of wholeness and peace. He has you securely in His loving care, and He will never let you go.

Another part of the journey toward healing involves clearing out clutter to make space for new beginnings. Are you still holding onto mementos and memories from past relationships? It's time to declutter and prepare for what lies ahead. Imagine going shopping for a brand-new wardrobe.

Before filling it with fresh, stylish pieces, you'd clean out your closet, right? You'd make room for the new by letting go of items that no longer fit or suit your current style. The same principle applies to your emotional life. Look inside your emotional closet. Are you storing old love letters, photos, or gifts from past relationships? Since these items no longer serve you or your future, it's time to let them go. Anything that might cause discomfort or hinder your ability to fully embrace a new relationship should be cleared out. It's about creating space for growth and new possibilities.

Study Guide: Chapter 8: Healing from Emotional Trauma

This chapter offers support and encouragement to women who have experienced emotional trauma and long for healing.

Key Points:

- Trauma is real, and its effects can be deep, but healing is possible.
- God desires complete healing for you and offers His love and support.
- Healing is a journey, not a destination, requiring time and courage.
- Therapy and Holy Spirit-led guidance can be invaluable resources.
- Acknowledge your pain, don't suppress it.
- Forgive those who hurt you, not for them, but for yourself.
- Be patient with yourself; healing is not linear.
- God is with you, offering comfort, guidance, and restoration.
- Declutter your emotional life to make room for new beginnings.

Reflection and Discussion Questions:

1.   How can you create a safe space to acknowledge and process your pain?

2.   What are ways the concept of forgiveness can set you free?

_____

_____

_____

_____

3.   What are some ways to practice self-compassion during healing?

_____

_____

_____

_____

4.   How can you incorporate prayer and scripture into your healing journey?

_____

_____

_____

_____

5.   What steps can you take to declutter your emotional life and move forward?

_____

_____

_____

_____

Activities:

- **Journaling**: Write about your emotions, experiences, and the impact of past hurts.
- **Gratitude Practice**: Focus on the good things in your life to cultivate positivity.
- **Letting Go**: Release physical reminders of past relationships.
- **Self-Care Practices**: Develop healthy practices that nurture your body, mind, and spirit.

Remember:

- Healing is a brave choice. You are worthy of love, happiness, and healthy relationships.
- God's love is unconditional, and He walks beside you through every step of your journey.
- Embrace forgiveness as a gift to yourself, allowing you to move forward with an open heart.

Chapter 9
Dating With Purpose

While you're single, embrace this season as a unique opportunity to deepen your relationship with God. It's a time where distractions are minimized, allowing for uninterrupted communion with Him. Make the most of it by spending quality time in His presence. Meeting someone new often requires intentional effort. Whether it's through social gatherings, hobbies, or even dating apps, putting yourself out there increases your chances of connecting with someone special. Engaging in activities you enjoy can naturally lead to meeting like-minded individuals who share your interests. While traditionally it's seen as the man's role to initiate, there's nothing wrong with a woman initiating conversation or expressing interest in a respectful manner. You might notice that some guys aren't so bold when it comes to approaching women. The kind of guy you're hoping to meet might not be the type to make the first move often. On the other hand, those who are too smooth at it might already be juggling a few other interests. It's totally fine to show your interest to a guy, but once you've done that, let him take the lead. The responsibility of pursuit lies with him thereafter. If you feel a connection, reciprocate accordingly. Avoid playing games or acting disinterested. Conversely, if you're not interested, communicate your feelings honestly and respectfully. Ghosting or prolonging relationships that lack potential is unproductive and unfair to both parties.

You might wonder, how long should you date someone before things get serious? Well, there's no one-size-fits-all answer to that question. It varies from person to person and situation to situation. But regardless of the timeline, the intention behind the dating should be clear from the start. If you're dating with the goal of marriage, make sure he knows that. Don't be afraid to be upfront about your intentions. If that scares him off, then maybe it's best to let him go. It's surprising how some people can be a month into dating and know all sorts of personal details about each other, down to the name of their childhood dog, and their granny's favorite dessert, yet still not know fundamental things like their beliefs. That doesn't make sense, does it? You should be open about who you are and what you want right from the beginning. And by "what you want," I don't mean reciting a laundry list of traits you expect in a partner. Instead, let him reveal his true self, and see if he aligns with your values and desires naturally.

When starting a relationship with someone, it's crucial to set healthy boundaries. Don't underestimate the power of temptation by putting yourself in compromising situations. And don't let your newfound relationship derail the disciplines you've established for yourself. For example, if you've set aside quiet time with God, continue to honor that commitment even as you enter a relationship. Your hobbies and routines are important aspects of your life; they shouldn't be sidelined by a new relationship. Remember, a man should enhance your life, not dictate it. It's also essential to have a solid support system and accountability structure in place. Surround yourself with people who will hold you accountable and speak the truth into your life. If you lack a father figure who can provide godly counsel regarding your relationship, seek guidance from someone you trust, such as a pastor or mentor. The Bible emphasizes the importance of seeking wise counsel (Proverbs 24:6-7), especially when making significant life decisions like choosing a partner. After all, who you decide to journey through life with is one of the most crucial decisions you'll ever make, second only to choosing God.

Study Guide: Chapter 9: Dating with Purpose
This chapter explores navigating singleness with a purpose, focusing on deepening your relationship with God while preparing for a future relationship.

Key Points:

- Singleness is an opportunity to build a strong foundation with God.
- Pursue intentional time with God through prayer, worship, and scripture.
- Expand your social circle and engage in activities you enjoy.
- Initiate connections with potential partners respectfully.
- Communicate your dating goals and expectations clearly.
- Prioritize your values and establish Godly disciplines.
- Maintain healthy boundaries and a strong support system.
- Seek guidance from mentors when making important decisions.

Reflection and Discussion Questions:

1.   How can you dedicate more time for your relationship with God while single?

2.   What are your interests and hobbies? How can you use them to connect with others?

_____

_____

_____

_____

3.   What qualities do you seek in a potential partner?

_____

_____

_____

_____

4.   How can you be upfront about your dating goals without coming across as pushy?

_____

_____

_____

_____

5.	What are some examples of healthy boundaries in a dating relationship?

_____

_____

_____

_____

6.	Who are the people in your life who can offer Godly counsel?

_____

_____

_____

_____

Activities:

- **Develop a Daily Devotional Plan**: Set aside dedicated time for prayer and scripture reading.
- **Expand Your Social Circle**: Join clubs or groups related to your interests.
- **Practice Honest Communication**: Role-play with your group/friend how you'd express yourself in certain dating scenarios.
- **Identify Your Boundaries**: Discuss situations where boundaries might be challenged.
- **Mentorship Meeting**: Schedule a meeting with a trusted mentor to discuss your dating journey.

Remember:

- Singleness is a valuable season for personal growth and spiritual development.
- Seek a partner who complements your faith and life goals.
- Prioritize clear communication and mutual respect while dating.
- Surround yourself with positive influences who support your values.

Conclusion

As we come to the end of this journey together, I want to leave you with a few final thoughts. This book has taken us through a myriad of topics, from rethinking marriage to embracing singleness as a gift, from healing emotional wounds to dating with purpose. This book has shattered the traditional mold of "wife-in-waiting" narratives. We've tossed out the idea of passive expectation and embraced an active journey of self-discovery and transformation; one that has challenged us to examine our beliefs, confront our fears, and embrace the fullness of who we are in Christ. At its core, this book is about more than just preparing for marriage or navigating the complexities of singleness. It's about becoming whole within us, recognizing that true partnership begins with two complete individuals coming together in unity. Wholeness precedes a healthy marriage. No one should be burdened with the task of filling a void within the other. Instead, we should seek partners who complement and enhance the amazing people we already are; individuals who cheer us on and make our strengths shine even brighter.

Throughout these pages, we've explored the importance of preparation during the single season, not just for the wedding day, but for the marriage itself. Singleness isn't a waiting game; it's a training ground. We've challenged traditional notions of waiting for a spouse and instead embraced singleness as an opportunity for growth, self-discovery, and deepening our relationship with God. And as we prepare for marriage, we've recognized that it's not the finish line, but rather the beginning of a lifelong journey of learning and growth together. Marriage, as we've discovered, is also like a training ground; a place where we learn and grow, where we stumble and make mistakes, but where we also extend grace to one another and ourselves. It's a journey of intimacy and vulnerability, of confronting our flaws and embracing our strengths. And through it all, we're reminded of the importance of extending grace, both to our partners and to ourselves.

This journey of self-discovery isn't meant to be solitary. Gather your friends, your church community, or fellow readers to create a support system. Remember, transformation often requires stepping outside your comfort zone and challenging the status quo. The accompanying study guide is more than supplementary; it's a vital tool. Engage with its questions, grapple with the discomfort, and allow yourself to be transformed. Through honest reflection and introspection, you'll discover not only a deeper understanding of the book's message, but also profound insights about yourself.

As we close this chapter, I want to encourage you to continue this journey of self-discovery and transformation. Embrace the challenges, lean into the discomfort, and trust that God is with you every step of the way. And as you navigate the ups and downs of life, remember the words of Philippians 1:6: "Being confident of this, that he who began a good work in you will carry it on to completion until the day of Christ Jesus."

Thank you for joining me on this journey. May you continue to grow in wisdom, grace, and love, and may your life be a testimony to the transformative power of God's grace.

Prayer for Your Husband

Father, I am committed to live pure and holy. I humble myself with fasting and prayer to put to death any part of me that is worldly. I declare that I am free from immorality, impurity, evil desires, and greed. Convict my heart and remind me that sin is not just about breaking the rules, but it breaks your heart when I open the door for hurt and pain to come upon me. I am submitting to you every area of my life. Heal my broken heart and bind up my wounds. Create in me a clean heart and renew a steadfast spirit within me. I am grateful for my season of singleness. Teach me and prepare me to be the Godly wife you desire me to be. Grace me to be a wife. Holy Spirit, be a shield and guard the purity of my senses. Protect and triumph over the images that have entered my mind. In a world of many voices, make your voice clear as I incline my ears to hear your voice. Let my words be proof that my heart is filled with you. As you are bringing myself and my husband into alignment, I pray that we are brought together by noble purpose, and not fleshly desires. I pray that our union be a testimony for so many, giving you all the Glory. What you are bringing together, no man can separate. Marriage is your design and your will for our lives, so Father, I call forth my Kingdom husband. Direct our steps to lead to one another. I bind and cast down any spirit of delay. I bind and cast down any counterfeit that would come to deceive us. Continue to walk with us and guide us as we live uncompromised lives submitted to you. In Jesus name, Amen.

www.ingramcontent.com/pod-product-compliance
Lightning Source LLC
Chambersburg PA
CBHW070758120626
46557CB00002B/646